Fiction Reading, grammar and vocabulary • Student book page

A Now answer these questions about the text.

1 Why did Abdullah's mum want him to work hard at school?
_____

2 Do you think Abdullah's grandfather is sad that Abdullah didn't catch a butterfly that day? How do you know?
_____

3 Why was Abdullah sad that he hadn't caught the butterfly?
_____

B Find verbs in the text, which match the following definitions, and fill in the spaces. You might need a dictionary to help you.

1 _____ to stop something and grasp it.

2 _____ to work on school work.

3 _____ to feel you might get something you want.

4 _____ to twist thread or thin pieces of wood together.

1 Find four adjectives in the text.

_____ _____ _____ _____

2 Now use the adjectives above to complete these sentences.

  a Abdullah is happy to go to English classes because they are his _____ lessons.

  b The scorpion was too _____ to fit in the jar.

  c Abdullah's mother works very hard in the _____ workshop.

  d When she was younger, she was a very _____ woman.

COPYRIGHT OXFORD UNIVERSITY PRESS 2013. PHOTOCOPYING PROHIBITED

Nouns, adjectives and verbs

A Put the words in the correct order to make sentences. Add capital letters and full stops.

1 singing are bus three on children the little
_____

2 Emilia window out looks of the dirty
_____

3 sees playing some a water dog Jamal in happy
_____

4 is book a reading Jade long
_____

B Use words from the sentences above to complete these lists.

nouns	proper nouns	adjectives	verbs
bus	Emilia	long	singing
_____	_____	_____	_____
_____	_____	_____	_____
_____	_____	_____	_____
_____			

Fiction Grammar and vocabulary • Student book pages 16 and 17

C Word search

Find 5 nouns, 5 proper nouns, 5 adjectives and 5 verbs.
Use the clues below to help you.

s	c	r	e	e	p	i	n	g	a	j
g	r	a	b	b	e	d	f	e	e	u
c	a	i	r	o	b	b	e	r	r	i
o	s	h	r	i	e	k	e	d	o	c
l	h	a	r	d	n	e	w	a	p	y
d	i	z	s	u	g	a	r	s	l	c
o	n	i	o	n	l	c	e	h	a	l
i	g	j	a	m	a	i	c	a	n	e
f	i	r	e	e	n	g	i	n	e	a
m	a	r	l	a	d	a	v	i	d	n

Nouns
1 f___ e_____
2 o_____
3 a_____
4 s____
5 r_____

Proper nouns
1 J_____
2 C____
3 M____
4 E_____
5 D____

Verbs
1 c____ing
2 c____ing
3 g____ed
4 d___
5 sh____ed

Adjectives
1 n__
2 h___
3 c___
4 j____
5 c____

COPYRIGHT OXFORD UNIVERSITY PRESS 2013. PHOTOCOPYING PROHIBITED

Fiction Grammar and vocabulary • Student book page 18

Powerful verbs

A Draw lines to connect these powerful verbs with the correct definition.

snatch — cry sadly
sob — eat quickly
beam — move slowly
creep — smile happily
gobble — take suddenly

B Make a list of some verbs that have the same meaning as the verbs in the clouds but are more interesting. One example has been given for you.

walk — creep
run — dash
eat — gobble

C Write these sentences again using more interesting verbs than 'walk', 'run' and 'eat'.

1 A cat walked up behind a bird.

2 The man is running for the bus.

3 Lucy ate her breakfast hungrily.

6   COPYRIGHT OXFORD UNIVERSITY PRESS 2013. PHOTOCOPYING PROHIBITED

Fiction Assessment

Self-assessment on my learning
Unit 1 Home and school

Name _____

Date _____

☺ I understand and can do this well.

😐 I understand but I am not confident.

☹ I don't understand and find this difficult.

Learning objective	☺	😐	☹
Reading fiction skills			
I can find the meaning of unknown words by looking at the words around them.			
I can answer questions by reading a passage and finding the information I need.			
I can understand that characters in stories think one thing, but say a different thing to what they think.			
Writing skills			
I can choose powerful words which make a sentence more exciting.			
I understand how choosing certain words can increase meaning.			
Language skills			
I can collect examples of nouns, verbs and adjectives and use them correctly.			

I would like more help with _____

_____

_____

2 Find out how!

Signs and instructions

A Look at the signs below. Match each sign with a place where you would see it.

Please remain seated until your name is called	60 km	Do not touch!
		Flight boarding

| Pens
Pencils
Crayons
Felt-tips | Raspberries
250 grams | No feeding the animals |
| | | Keep dogs on a lead |

1 In a doctor's surgery
2 Driving along a road
3 In a school classroom
4 In an airport
5 In a supermarket
6 In a museum
7 In a park
8 In a zoo

Non-fiction Reading • Student book pages 26, 27 and 30

1 Imagine that you are going to make a cup of tea. Write a list of all the things that you will need.

- a cup
- _____
- _____
- _____

- _____
- _____
- _____

2 Here are the instructions to make the tea, but they are not in the correct order. Give the instructions a number and put them in the right order.

- Put the teabag in the cup ____
- Stir and leave for one minute ____
- Find a clean cup ____
- Remove the teabag ____
- Take a teabag ____
- Add milk or sugar to the tea ____
- Boil some water ____
- Pour the boiled water into the cup ____

C Now rewrite the instructions in the correct order in a paragraph. Use the words below to connect the sentences and to show which order the instructions come in.

first   lastly   then   and   next   after that   and

Example: **First,** find a clean cup **and** take a teabag. **Then**…

_____
_____
_____
_____

Non-fiction Grammar and vocabulary • Student book pages 29, 32 and 33

Verbs

A Find the 12 hidden verbs that can be used in instructions.

m	i	x	z	x	h	t
a	o	c	i	l	o	a
k	p	u	t	f	l	k
e	m	t	c	k	d	e
f	a	s	t	e	n	p
o	d	i	e	e	o	o
l	d	i	u	p	o	u
d	s	t	i	r	g	r

1 take
2 h_____
3 p_____
4 k_____
5 c_____
6 m_____
7 p_____
8 m_____
9 a_____
10 f_____
11 f_____
12 s_____

B Use some of the verbs above to complete these instructions.

1 _____ your scissors and carefully _____ along the dotted line.

2 _____ off the grass!

3 _____ the milk into the mixture and _____ with a wooden spoon.

C Use the pairs of verbs below to write an instruction.

Example: **Take** two colours and **mix** them together.

1 put/mix _____

2 cut/glue _____

3 take/fold _____

10 COPYRIGHT OXFORD UNIVERSITY PRESS 2013. PHOTOCOPYING PROHIBITED

Non-fiction Grammar and punctuation • Student book pages 32 and 33

Sentences and questions

A Put these words into the correct order to make a sentence. Add the correct punctuation.

1 has brothers older Theo two
_____

2 another can have biscuit I ?
_____

3 Misaki school with to walk I
_____

4 cinema we to see to went the film a
_____

B Add the correct question word to complete these questions.

what   when   where   who   why

1 _____ do you live?
2 _____ does it look like?
3 _____ is your birthday?
4 _____ are you wearing two hats?
5 _____ is going to the park with you?

C Choose two of the questions words from above and write your own questions. Don't forget to use the correct punctuation.

1 _____
2 _____

Non-fiction Grammar and spelling • Student book pages 34 and 35

Tenses

A Choose the correct tenses to complete these sentences.
1. He **(was reading/reads)** his book every morning.
2. Nathan **(puts on/put on)** his coat because he was going outside.
3. Malik **(likes/liked)** watching football on TV.
4. Today Lisa **(wore/is wearing)** her favourite blue dress.
5. She **(knew/was knowing)** the answer to the teacher's question.

B Put the verbs in the correct tense.
1. Last night, I _____ **(watch)** a programme about whales.
2. Elephants _____ **(live)** in Africa.
3. We always _____ **(visit)** my granny on Saturdays.
4. Kassar _____ **(score)** three goals in the football match.
5. Peter _____ **(finish)** his homework quickly so he could go out to play.

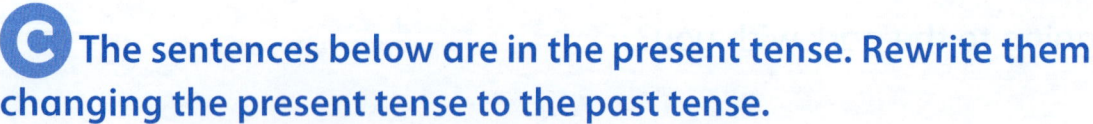

C The sentences below are in the present tense. Rewrite them changing the present tense to the past tense.
1. She looks everywhere for her dancing shoes.
_____
2. He walks to school every morning.
_____
3. He isn't at home because he is playing football in the park.
_____

Non-fiction Assessment

Self-assessment on my learning

Unit 2 Find out how!

Name _____

Date _____

☺ I understand and can do this well.

😐 I understand but I am not confident.

☹ I don't understand and find this difficult.

Learning objective	☺	😐	☹
Reading non-fiction skills			
I can read and follow instructions.			
I can write instructions in order and with connecting words.			
I think about the language used in written instructions and signs.			
Writing skills			
I can choose the right style for whatever I am writing.			
I think about how information is written on a page.			
I can choose the correct tense.			
Language skills			
I can find examples of nouns, verbs and adjectives and use them correctly.			
I understand that I need to use a verb in a sentence.			

I would like more help with _____

_____

_____

3 Our sensational senses

Poetry Reading • Student book pages 42, 43 and 46

Fishes' Evening Song

Read this sound poem out loud.

Flip flop,
Flip flap,
Slip slap,
Lip lap;
Water sounds,
Soothing sounds.
We fan our fins
As we lie
Resting here
Eye to eye.
Water falls
Drop by drop,
Plip plop,
Drip drop.

Plink plunk,
Splash splish;
Fish fins fan,
Fish tails swish,
Swush, swash, swish.
This we wish…
Water cold,
Water clear,
Water smooth,
Just to soothe
Sleepy fish.

Dahlov Ipcar

Poetry Reading • Student book pages 41, 42, 43 and 46

A Answer the comprehension questions below about the poem.

1 Look at lines 1–5 of the poem. Which words describe the sound of water?
   _____

2 Who or what is 'we' in lines 7 and 8 of the poem? How do you know this?
   _____
   _____

3 Some of the words are made-up words. Find the made-up words and write them here. Use a dictionary to help you.
   _____
   _____

B Some words sound like the thing that they are describing. *Example:* 'whoosh' could describe a firework going through the air.

Find the words in the poem that describe the sound of:

1 water dropping _____

2 a fish moving _____

C Make a list of words to describe as many sounds as you can think of that you might hear at the seaside. You can make some of them up if you want to!

Real words	Made-up words
splash	splosh
_____	_____
_____	_____
_____	_____
_____	_____

COPYRIGHT OXFORD UNIVERSITY PRESS 2013. PHOTOCOPYING PROHIBITED

Poetry Vocabulary and spelling • Student book pages 48 and 49

Prefixes

A Write the opposite meaning to the words in the cloud using either the prefix 'un-' or 'dis-'.

___respect   ___kind   ___tidy   ___appear   ___lucky

___dress   ___comfort   ___like   ___necessary   ___order

___trust   ___comfortable   ___popular

Choose 5 of the words above and use each of them in a sentence.

1 _____
2 _____
3 _____
4 _____
5 _____

B Circle the correct words to match the definitions.

1 to make new plans   **prearrange/rearrange**
2 to make plans beforehand   **prearrange/rearrange**
3 to heat beforehand   **preheat/reheat**
4 to reduce the value   **prevalue/devalue**
5 to heat again   **preheat/reheat**
6 to remove bones   **rebone/debone**
7 to change a booking   **rebook/debook**

16 COPYRIGHT OXFORD UNIVERSITY PRESS 2013. PHOTOCOPYING PROHIBITED

Poetry Vocabulary and spelling • Student book pages 48 and 49

More prefixes

A Write a definition for these words. You can use a dictionary to help you.

refill _____

retake _____

unhook _____

readdress _____

precook _____

Now write a sentence using each of the words.

1 _____
2 _____
3 _____
4 _____
5 _____

B Choose the correct word from the list below to complete the sentences.

| deactivate | recapture | declined | preheat | rechargeable |

1 We use _____ batteries, which are more environmentally friendly.

2 You will need to _____ the oven before cooking the cake.

3 Miso's rabbit escaped from its cage, but his mum managed to _____ it.

4 The spy had to quickly _____ the bomb before it went off.

5 Mum _____ the party invite because dad was late home from work.

COPYRIGHT OXFORD UNIVERSITY PRESS 2013. PHOTOCOPYING PROHIBITED

Poetry Writing • Student book pages 41, 42, 43, 44 and 45

Writing poems

A

1 At the beginning of this unit, you wrote a list of sounds you might hear at the seaside. Do any of your words sound like the things they describe?
Example: crashing waves, squawking seagulls.

Write some more of your own examples here.

_____

2 In the 'Fishes' Evening Song' poem, the writer sometimes repeats the first letter (or first sound) of the words for effect.

Example: plink plunk, splash splish, fish fins fan. **Can you find some other examples of this in the poem?**

_____

B The writer also uses rhyming words too. Words rhyme when they have the same ending sound.

Example: 'clock' and 'sock' which have the same spelling, or 'door' and 'saw' which have different spellings but the same sound.

1 Find a word in the poem which rhymes with these words.

slap _____   lie _____   drop _____   smooth _____

2 Find 3 words in the poem which rhyme with the word 'fish'.

_____ _____ _____

C Write your own short poem describing the seaside or another place of your choice. Include some rhyming words and think about the things you might see, feel, hear, smell and taste.

_____
_____
_____
_____

Poetry Assessment

Self-assessment on my learning

Unit 3 Our sensational senses

Name _____

Date _____

☺ I understand and can do this well.

😐 I understand but I am not confident.

☹ I don't understand and find this difficult.

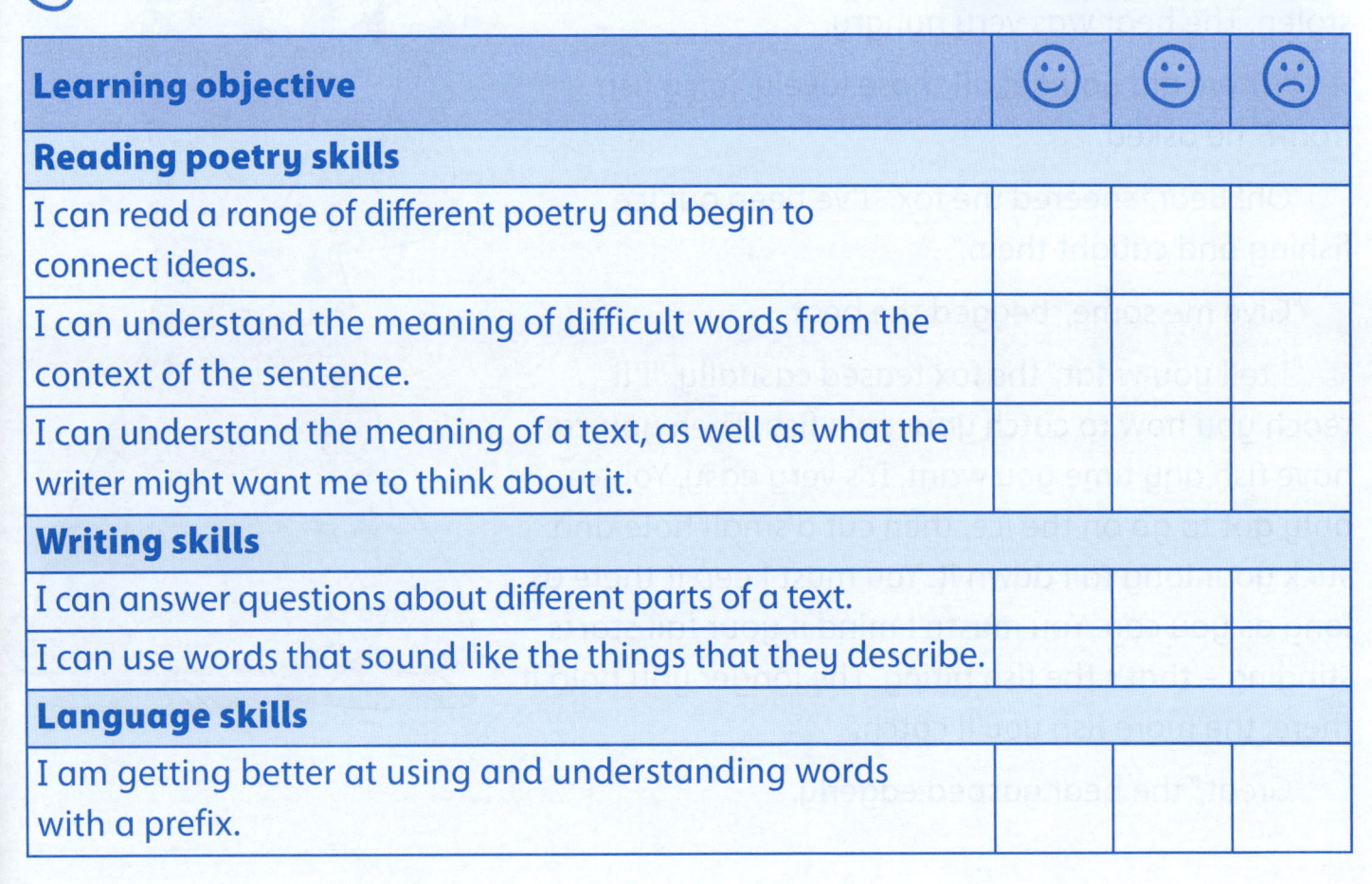

Learning objective	☺	😐	☹
Reading poetry skills			
I can read a range of different poetry and begin to connect ideas.			
I can understand the meaning of difficult words from the context of the sentence.			
I can understand the meaning of a text, as well as what the writer might want me to think about it.			
Writing skills			
I can answer questions about different parts of a text.			
I can use words that sound like the things that they describe.			
Language skills			
I am getting better at using and understanding words with a prefix.			

I would like more help with _____

_____

_____

4 Traditional tales

Fiction Reading • Student book pages 56, 57 and 60

Why the Bear is Stumpy-tailed

Read this passage from a Norwegian traditional tale.

Once upon a time there was a bear. Back in those days, the bear had a beautiful, long tail and he was very proud of it. One icy cold day the bear met a fox, who came slinking along with a string of fish he had stolen. The bear was very hungry.

"Where did you get all those lovely, juicy fish from?" he asked.

"Oh! Bear," sneered the fox, "I've been out ice fishing and caught them."

"Give me some," begged the bear.

"I tell you what," the fox teased casually, "I'll teach you how to catch your own fish. Then you can have fish any time you want. It's very easy. You've only got to go on the ice, then cut a small hole and stick your long tail down it. You must keep it there as long as you can. You mustn't mind if your tail starts stinging – that's the fish biting. The longer you hold it there, the more fish you'll catch."

"Great," the bear gasped eagerly.

Fiction Reading • Student book pages 56, 57 and 60

A Draw lines to match the words from the story with their correct definitions. Use a dictionary to help you. The first one has been done as an example.

stumpy   not serious
to slink   feel a prick of sharp pain
eagerly   walk in a slow, bendy way
casual   enthusiastically
to sting   short and thick

B Answer the questions using words and phrases from the story to help you.

1 Do you think the fox is telling the truth about catching the fish he is carrying? Explain your answer.
_____
2 What does the fox say will make the bear's tail hurt in the frozen water?
_____
3 What do you think will make the bear's tail hurt in the frozen water?
_____
4 Why do you think the bear is happy to believe the fox's story?
_____

1 Look at the story again. Find three verbs that have been used instead of the word 'said'. _____ _____ _____

2 Write your own sentences using these verbs. You might need to look some of them up in your dictionary.

• _____

• _____

• _____

COPYRIGHT OXFORD UNIVERSITY PRESS 2013. PHOTOCOPYING PROHIBITED

Synonyms and more interesting words for 'said'

A These words are all synonyms for 'said'. Use a dictionary to find out what they mean and then put each word in the correct box. Some words might go in more than one box. *Example:* 'barked' could go in 'said loudly' or 'said angrily'.

bawled	whimpered	mumbled	moaned	bellowed
murmured	grunted	roared	muttered	sighed
raved	screamed	yelled	barked	groaned
thundered	whispered	screeched	wailed	howled

'said loudly' | 'said softly' | 'said angrily'

barked | | barked

B Use one of the words above to complete these sentences.

1 "Get out of my room now!" _____ my brother angrily.
2 "I've hurt my toe," _____ Sofia miserably.
3 "Do you want to know my secret?" _____ Lena.

More synonyms

A Use a thesaurus to find synonyms for the words below.

kind _____   unhappy _____   frightened _____

funny _____   hungry _____   clever _____

B Match a word from the first box with a synonym in the second box.

Example: windy = blustery

windy	beautiful	angry	mumbled	bellowed	stunning
shouted	whispered	brown	blustery	chestnut	ancient
old	cold	hot	scorching	enraged	chilly

C Replace the word 'nice' in these sentences with a more interesting synonym.

1 Tessa has (nice) _____ long, blonde hair.

2 The dinner mum cooked was (nice) _____.

3 Syed is a really (nice) _____ and polite boy.

4 My uncle has a really (nice) _____ new car.

5 It was very (nice) _____ of the girl to give the old lady her seat.

6 Our house is on a (nice) _____ street.

Speech marks and punctuation

A Add the speech marks and the correct punctuation to these conversations.

Have you done your homework Milan asked the teacher

Yes he replied but I left it at home

Sit down my mother barked angrily

I can't I replied the chair is broken

Are you playing football after school today Luca asked

No replied Diego I have to go to the dentist

B Write what you think Clara says in the following dialogue with her neighbour. Don't forget to use the correct punctuation.

"Hi Clara, are you doing anything nice this weekend?" asked Mrs Khan.

_____

"Is it really? How old will you be?" replied Mrs Khan kindly.

_____

"Well, I never!" continued Mrs Khan. "Are you going to do anything special?"

_____

_____

"Oh, that's fantastic," beamed Mrs Khan.

Fiction Assessment

Self-assessment on my learning
Unit 4 Traditional tales

Name _____

Date _____

☺ I understand and can do this well.

😐 I understand but I am not confident.

☹ I don't understand and find this difficult.

Learning objective	☺	😐	☹
Reading fiction skills			
I can answer questions about different parts of a text.			
I can recognize different types of stories and story themes.			
I can understand the meaning of difficult words by looking at the words around them and the the sentences that they are in.			
Writing skills			
I can use exciting words that make a big impression on the reader.			
Language skills			
I can use synonyms for words that are used very often, like 'said'.			
I can use the correct vocabulary to begin and end a dialogue.			
I can use the correct punctuation and speech marks when using dialogue.			

I would like more help with _____

_____

_____

Keep in touch!

Letters

Read this letter and then answer the questions.

Dear Mr Cook,

I am writing to complain about the dreadful evening I spent at your restaurant last night.

My son and I were celebrating my 50th birthday. All we wanted was a peaceful evening, eating a delightful meal. However, next to us there was a family with young children making a frightful noise. When I complained, the waiter was useless as he was so fearful of upsetting the parents.

The food was twenty minutes late and it was completely tasteless.

I would therefore be grateful if you consider how you can improve your service in the future.

Yours sincerely,

Mrs B. Brown

Non-fiction Reading, vocabulary and spelling • Student book pages 72, 73, 76, 78 and 79

Comprehension and the suffixes -ful, -less

A Tick one statement that you know is true from Mrs Brown's letter.

☐ The restaurant was very quiet.
☐ The waiter didn't care if he upset the children's parents.
☐ The food tasted really terrible.
☐ The food arrived on time.
☐ Mrs Brown would like some changes to be made to make the restaurant service better.

B Answer the questions about the letter.

1 What is the purpose of this letter?
_____

2 Is it an informal or formal letter? How do you know?
_____

C

1 Make a list of all the words with suffixes used in the letter. Then write another word with the same meaning next to the suffix word. The first one has been done for you.

dreadful _____   terrible _____
_____   _____
_____   _____
_____   _____
_____   _____
_____   _____

2 Now make a sentence using these words.
• successful _____
• endless _____

COPYRIGHT OXFORD UNIVERSITY PRESS 2013. PHOTOCOPYING PROHIBITED

Non-fiction Vocabulary and spelling • Student book pages 78 and 79

More suffixes

Don't forget to change 'y' to 'i'.

A Read the definitions below and then fill in the missing suffix. The first one has been done for you.

-less or **-ful**

showing good taste	taste**ful**
caring or considerate	thought_____
having no money at all	penny_____
not able to relax	rest_____
very valuable	price_____
to feel upset and angry	resent_____
to have lots of use	use_____
to be very strong	power_____

B The suffix -ly is often added to make adverbs. Adverbs describe how something is done. Add -ly to the following lists of words.

List 1	List 2	List 3
careful **carefully**	horrible **horribly**	easy **easily**
bad_____	terrible_____	merry_____
tight_____	idle_____	healthy_____
slow_____	feeble_____	angry_____
clever_____	gentle_____	messy_____

C Read the rules below. Which rule applies to lists 1, 2 and 3 above?

List _____ you take away the **e** from the end of the word and add **-ly**

List _____ you change the **y** at the end of the word to i then add **-ly**

List _____ you simply add **-ly**

28 COPYRIGHT OXFORD UNIVERSITY PRESS 2013. PHOTOCOPYING PROHIBITED

Singular and plural nouns

 A Add 's' or 'es' to the following singular nouns to make them plural.

church__   table__   watch__   brush__
house__   axe__   class__   dish__
wax__   bench__   chair__   car__
kiss__   beach__   eyelash__   dress__
rock__   hand__   shoe__   cushion__
address__   match__   flash__   floor__
six__   pencil__   spoon__   tax__

 B

1 What are the plurals of these irregular nouns?

mouse ⇒ _____   man ⇒ _____   child ⇒ _____
sheep ⇒ _____   woman ⇒ _____ person ⇒ _____

2 Now use three of these plural nouns to write interesting sentences of your own.
Example: The mice ate so much cheese that they were full up!

• _____

• _____

• _____

Apostrophes

A Read Mia's letter to her granny and add the missing apostrophes.

B Answer the questions about the letter.

1 What is the purpose of this letter?
_____
_____
_____

2 Is it a formal or an informal letter? How do you know?
_____
_____
_____
_____

Hi Granny,

Were having a great time here in Austria. Ive been skiing every day and cant believe how much Ive improved. I know I shouldnt show off but I think Im even better than Dad now. Hell never admit it though! Were coming home late on Wednesday, so I wont see you until Thursday.

Bye,
Mia

C Write the contractions of the following words.

Example: I have ⇒ I've

She will _____   Do not _____
Can not _____   I am _____
Was not _____   They would _____
Did not _____   Will not _____
Must not _____   He is _____

Non-fiction Assessment

Self-assessment on my learning
Unit 5 Keep in touch!

Name _____

Date _____

☺ I understand and can do this well.

😐 I understand but I am not confident.

☹ I don't understand and find this difficult.

Learning objective	☺	😐	☹
Reading non-fiction skills			
I can read a text and understand what its main purpose is.			
I can scan a passage to find specific information to answer questions.			
Writing skills			
I can understand who I am writing a letter to, and for what reason.			
I can use the correct formal or informal style depending on who I am writing to.			
Language skills			
I can recognize and use different suffixes and prefixes.			
I can use apostrophes in words that have been shortened.			

I would like more help with _____

_____

_____

COPYRIGHT OXFORD UNIVERSITY PRESS 2013. PHOTOCOPYING PROHIBITED

Play scripts Writing • Student book pages 88, 89, 92

Sharing cultures

Coyote Steals the Sun

Read this extract from a Zuni legend about the sun and moon.

Long, long ago, when the world was still dark as there was no sun or moon yet in the sky, lived Coyote. Coyote was a terrible hunter, which he blamed on the darkness. He never managed to catch anything so he was always hungry.

One day he saw Eagle hunting rabbits. Eagle was such a good hunter that he was able to catch many more rabbits than he could possibly eat. Coyote immediately thought that if he could hunt with Eagle then he would never be hungry again.

Coyote asked Eagle if they could join together saying that two were surely always better than one. Eagle agreed, so they started to hunt together.

Play scripts Writing • Student book pages 50, 51, 88, 89 and 92

A Below is the 'Coyote Steals the Sun' story but it is written as a play script. Use the story on page 32 to complete the dialogue in your own words.

> Look back at pages 50 and 51 of your Student Book for tips.

Narrator: Long, long ago, when the world was still in darkness as there was no moon or sun yet in the sky, lived Coyote.

Coyote: *(sitting miserably in almost complete darkness)* Oh, why am I such a terrible _____? I never manage _____ and I'm always _____. If only it wasn't so so _____. Look, *(points sadly)* there is _____ hunting. He is such a good _____. He can catch so many rabbits.

Hmm, *(smiles slyly as he thinks)* I have a plan. If I could only hunt with Eagle then _____ again.

(He calls out) Friend!

(Eagle comes over to where Coyote is sitting.)

B Continue the dialogue by imagining what Coyote and Eagle say to each other in this next part of the story. Include the stage directions.

Eagle and Coyote went hunting together many times, but each time it was the same. Eagle caught a rabbit, Coyote caught nothing. Though he caught nothing, Coyote was greedy and ate twice as much as Eagle. Eagle became tired of hunting for the greedy Coyote. He was cross with Coyote for being such a useless hunter and told him he must try harder.

Coyote: _____

_____

Eagle: _____

_____

Alphabetical ordering and irregular verbs

A Put the following words in alphabetical order.

1 coyote   chop   custom   carry   _____
2 eagle   excuse   essay   equal   _____
3 dig   dog   dug   deep   _____
4 indeed   invent   inform   increase _____

B The verb 'to be' is an irregular verb. Choose the past tense of the verb to fill the gaps.

1 The class _____ waiting for lunchtime to arrive.
2 Rana _____ talking to the teacher at her desk.
3 Kia _____ finishing her class work.
4 She _____ sitting next to Lea.
5 They _____ both wearing hairbands.
6 Joshi and Rao _____ playing chess.
7 I _____ reading a book quietly.
8 Finally, the bell went and the class _____ able to go outside.

C Change these sentences from the past to the present tense.

1 David and Marek were talking about their homework at the bus stop.
   _____

2 I was running very fast because I wanted to catch up with Laura and Maria.
   _____

3 Theo's friends were waiting for him because he was looking for his coat.
   _____

More irregular verbs

A Use a dictionary to find the past tense of these irregular verbs.

awake _____   become _____   bring _____
bite _____   choose _____   freeze _____
know _____   eat _____   rise _____
catch _____   speak _____   hang _____

B Circle all the irregular verbs hidden in the word search. There are 26 altogether.

b	e	f	o	r	g	i	v	e	s
r	c	o	d	r	a	w	i	n	g
e	a	r	i	l	e	a	v	e	s
a	t	g	g	r	e	a	d	w	h
k	c	e	k	n	o	w	p	a	a
g	h	t	s	e	n	d	a	k	n
r	m	l	o	s	i	t	y	e	g
o	a	o	s	p	e	a	k	e	p
w	k	s	e	b	e	n	d	a	u
s	e	e	d	r	i	v	e	t	t

C Choose 5 of the irregular verbs and write a sentence using each one.

1 _____
2 _____
3 _____
4 _____
5 _____

Poetry Writing and spelling • Student book pages 95, 96 and 97

Writing poetry and the alphabet

Read this alphabet poem

My Best Friend

A She's so **amazing**
B She's so **bright**
C She's **clever** and sunny
D She's so **daring**
E She's so **exciting**
F She's **fabulous** and funny!

A Now answer the questions about the poem.

1 Which word is the same in each line?
_____

2 What do you notice about the bold words in the poem?
_____

3 What do you notice about lines 3 and 6 compared to the other lines?
_____
_____

B Write as many adjectives as you can to describe a friend or relative. The adjectives could be about their character or what they look like.
_____
_____

C Use your list of adjectives to write the next verse of the poem, describing a friend or relative.

G _____   J _____
H _____   K _____
I _____   L _____

36 COPYRIGHT OXFORD UNIVERSITY PRESS 2013. PHOTOCOPYING PROHIBITED

Poetry and play scripts Assessment

Self-assessment on my learning

Unit 6 Sharing cultures

Name _____

Date _____

☺ I understand and can do this well.

😐 I understand but I am not confident.

☹ I don't understand and find this difficult.

Learning objective	☺	😐	☹
Reading poetry and play scripts skills			
I can read a range of poems and play scripts.			
Writing skills			
I can write a poem.			
I am starting to use tenses properly.			
I can choose words to describe characters.			
I can write simple play scripts based on a story.			
Language skills			
I can use irregular forms of common verbs.			
I can organise words alphabetically.			
I can use a dictionary.			
I can choose and compare words to make my writing more descriptive or exciting.			

I would like more help with _____

_____

_____

It's a mystery!

Adventure and mystery stories

Precious and the Monkeys

Read this extract from Precious and the Monkeys.

They set off, following the path that wound down the hill. It was a narrow path and a winding one – here and there great boulders had rolled down the hill thousands of years ago and the path had to twist around these. In between the boulders, trees had grown up, their roots working their way through gaps in the stone. These trees made the places in between the rocks a cool **refuge** from the heat of the sun, and **sometimes** Precious would sit down there and rest on her way home. But these places were also good hiding places for snakes, and so you had to be **careful** or …

There was a **noise** off among the rocks, and they both gave a start.

"A snake?" whispered Poloko.

"Perhaps," said Precious. "Should we look?"

Poloko nodded. "Yes, but we must be careful."

They heard the noise again. This time Precious thought that it might be coming from the tree, and she **looked** up into the branches.

"There!" she said, pointing into the tangle of leaves.

Poloko looked up. He had expected to see a snake wound round one of the branches, but that was not what he **spotted**.

From *Precious and the Monkeys: Precious Ramotswe's Very First Case* by Alexander McCall Smith

Fiction Reading • Student book pages 102, 103 and 106

A Now answer these questions about the text.

1 Where did Precious sometimes rest on her way home?
   _____

2 Why did she have to be careful?
   _____

3 Where did Precious and Poloko think the noise was coming from?
   _____

4 The noise was not a snake. What do you think it might have been?
   _____

B Rewrite the sentences and replace the words in bold with 'he', 'they' or 'she'. Look back at the text to help you.

1 **Precious and Poloko** set off, following the path that wound down the hill.
   _____

2 There was a noise off among the rocks, and **Precious and Poloko** both gave a start.
   _____

3 "There!" **Precious** said, pointing into the tangle of leaves.
   _____

4 **Pokolo** had expected to see a snake wound round one of the branches.
   _____

C Look in your dictionary and find words that could replace the bold words in the text without changing the meaning of the sentences.

noise _____   careful _____

refuge _____   sometimes _____

looked _____   spotted _____

Fiction Vocabulary, spelling and grammar • Student book pages 108, 109, 110 and 111

Prefixes and pronouns

Prefixes

A Choose a word below to add to the prefixes to complete these sentences. You might need a dictionary to help you.

fiction   places   stop   ports   pilot

1 China **ex** _____ toys around the world
2 Lena ran **non** _____ all the way to school.
3 Gran always **mis** _____ her glasses so now she keeps them around her neck.
4 Florian's father is the **co** _____ of a jumbo jet.
5 Laura enjoys reading **non** _____, especially biographies.

B Write sentences using the following words.

1 nonsense _____
2 misleading _____

Pronouns

A Complete the sentences by adding the correct pronoun.

1 My mother told _____ to clean up my room.
2 He put _____ book in _____ bag.
3 As the children were being so loud, the teacher told _____ to be quieter.
4 Sofie gave _____ best friend a birthday present.
5 The boys put on their coats and then _____ went outside to play.
6 We were thirsty so Mum gave _____ a drink with _____ lunch.

B Make your own sentences using these pronouns.

1 she _____
2 them _____
3 it _____

Fiction Writing • Student book pages 112, 113, 114 and 115

Writing adventure stories

Read this adventure story.

Fred and Fred's little brother, Nathan, stood in the middle of the empty, ruined castle, outside the doorway to the completely black dungeon room.

"Nathan **dares** Fred to go in," whispered Nathan. Fred was shaking because Fred felt so terrified but Fred did not want Fred's little brother to know that Fred was frightened, so Fred grabbed Nathan's hand and said, "Fred will only go in if Nathan **comes** with Fred."

"OK. Nathan will come," said Nathan.

Together Fred and Nathan edged into the darkness. Fred felt Fred's heart beating so fast…. at least Nathan was with Fred. Further and further in Fred and Nathan went.

A Rewrite the story. Add the correct pronouns to replace the underlined words and then change the verb forms in bold if you need to.

Fiction Writing • Student book pages 112, 113, 114 and 115

B Read these statements about writing adventure stories and decide whether they are true or false. Draw a circle around the correct answer.

It is bad to describe the setting.	**True / False**
It is good to include dialogue.	**True / False**
It is good to always use short sentences.	**True / False**
It is bad to talk about how the main character feels.	**True / False**
It is good only to describe what the main character sees.	**True / False**
It is good to build up tension and to have some exciting action.	**True / False**
It is good to have a plot leading to a dramatic climax.	**True / False**
It is bad for the main hero to solve the problem at the end.	**True / False**
It is bad to use powerful adjectives.	**True / False**

C Write a more powerful adjective or verb next to the following words.

good _____
scary _____
horrible _____
smelly _____
shout _____
loud _____
crying _____
take _____
run _____

42 COPYRIGHT OXFORD UNIVERSITY PRESS 2013. PHOTOCOPYING PROHIBITED

Fiction Assessment

Self-assessment on my learning
Unit 7 It's a mystery!

Name _____

Date _____

☺ I understand and can do this well.

😐 I understand but I am not confident.

☹ I don't understand and find this difficult.

Learning objective	☺	😐	☹
Reading fiction skills			
I can understand the meaning of difficult words by looking at the words around them and at the sentences that they are in.			
I can identify the features of different types of stories.			
Writing skills			
I can use exciting words that make a big impression.			
I can use words to make my writing more descriptive.			
Language skills			
I can use a dictionary.			
I can use pronouns correctly in sentences.			
I can use correct verb forms with different pronouns.			
I can use a range of prefixes and suffixes.			

I would like more help with _____
_____
_____
_____

8 Our world

Non-chronological reports

A Read this report about the Arctic, then think of a title and three sub-headings. Write them in the spaces provided.

[Title] _____

[Sub-heading 1] _____

The Arctic is an area at the northern most part of the Earth. As well as the Arctic Ocean, this huge region includes parts of Russia, Greenland, Canada, the USA, Norway, Iceland, Sweden and Finland.

[Sub-heading 2] _____

The Arctic has cold winters and cool summers. The average winter temperature is −40 degrees Celsius. The coldest recorded temperature, measured in the Siberian village of Verkhoyansk, is −68 degrees Celsius. However, global warming is rapidly shrinking the amount of ice on the Arctic Ocean.

[Sub-heading 3] _____

People have lived in this frozen region since 2500 BC. The Inuit people living in the north west of Greenland are one of the most northern communities in the world. Most Inuit communities have settled along the coastline as these people depend on the sea to survive.

Non-Fiction Reading • Student book pages 118, 119 and 122

B Answer these questions using the information in the report.

1 The Arctic region includes parts of many different countries. Name five of them.
_____

2 What is the coldest temperature recorded in the Arctic region?
_____

3 Why is there less and less ice each year in the Arctic region?
_____

4 What is the name given to one of the groups of people who live in the most northern communities?
_____

5 Tick one box to show which statement is true.
☐ People living in the Arctic mostly live inland because it's warmer.
☐ The coldest temperature on record was measured in Greenland.
☐ People have lived in the Arctic region since 2500 BC.

C Does this report contain mostly facts or mostly opinions? Explain your answer.
_____
_____

Irregular verbs

A Complete these sentences with the correct verb form of 'to have' or 'to go'.

1 This morning Felix _____ to the dentist because he _____ toothache.

2 My neighbours _____ a lovely time when they _____ on holiday to Spain.

3 She _____ an uncle living there, so they _____ to Spain every year.

B Rewrite these sentences in the present tense.

1 Her family didn't have a car so she went to school on foot.
_____

2 I had an ice-cream when I went to the seaside.
_____

3 The boys had swimming lessons on Wednesdays so they went to the pool by bus.
_____
_____

C Use your own ideas to finish the sentences below. Use the verbs 'to have' or 'to go' in the past tense. Make the sentences as interesting as possible.

1 Jenna's hobby was skateboarding, so
_____

2 Mum doesn't like cooking, so
_____

3 Every Saturday, Pablo and his friends
_____

Simple and compound sentences

A Add the correct connective (and, so, but) to complete these compound sentences.

1 Alba was very tired, _____ she went to bed early.
2 I like most vegetables, _____ I don't like peas.
3 Emil likes literacy, _____ he likes numeracy.
4 Milan has been to India, _____ he has never been to Pakistan
5 Diego missed the bus, _____ he had to get a lift to school from his father.

B Join these sentences together using a connective to form a compound sentence.

1 Leo kicked the ball at the net. He didn't score a goal.
_____
2 Mathew didn't have anything to write with. I gave him a pencil.
_____
3 Julia likes ball games. She doesn't like running.
_____
4 Hassan loves running. He is the fastest boy in the class.
_____
5 I was feeling sick. The teacher phoned my mother to pick me up from school.
_____

C Complete these sentences with an idea of your own.

1 Lena wanted to go to the beach, so _____.
2 Louis has three brothers, but _____.
3 Patrik isn't very good at swimming, but _____.
4 My grandmother is a great cook, so _____.
5 Clara went to Portugal on holiday with her family and,
_____.

Clauses and commas

A Underline the main clause in the following sentences.

1 Before getting dressed, Ravi cleaned his teeth.
2 After school finished, Susan went to play at Millie's house.
3 When his mother came in the room, Khan was fast asleep.
4 Before slamming the door, Freda grabbed her coat.
5 When Enzo got up, he couldn't believe it was snowing!

B Complete these sentences with your own ideas and put a comma in the correct place.

1 Before picking Juan up from school his mother _____

2 Although Flora loved going to stay at her cousin's house she didn't _____

3 After Euan had finished his dinner he _____

4 When Alexander went to the park he was surprised to _____

5 As Norma was leaving the house her mother _____

C Look at the report on the Arctic again on page 44. Find two sentences where a subordinate clause has been used. Write them out below.

1 _____.
2 _____.

Non-fiction Assessment

Self-assessment on my learning

Unit 8 Our world

Name _____

Date _____

☺ I understand and can do this well.

😐 I understand but I am not confident.

☹ I don't understand and find this difficult.

Learning objective	☺	😐	☹
Reading non-fiction skills			
I can scan a passage to find specific information to answer questions.			
I can understand the main point of a text.			
Writing skills			
I can recognize the features of an information text.			
I am beginning to organize my writing in paragraphs.			
I am thinking about how information is set out on a page.			
Language skills			
I know irregular forms of common verbs.			
I can use simple, compound and complex sentences.			
I can use commas.			

I would like more help with _____

_____

_____

Poetry Vocabulary and spelling • Student book page 140

9 Why do we laugh?

Dictionary work

A Look up these verbs in a **dictionary** then draw a line to match them with their correct definition.

snigger — come down from the air suddenly
mutter — make a quick, sharp cry
snatch — laugh in a rude, disrespectful way
yelp — take suddenly
swoop — complain quietly

B Use the verbs above to complete this story. You will need to put the verbs in the past tense.

We were sitting in the park one sunny day having a family picnic. Suddenly a seagull _____ down from nowhere and _____ the cheese sandwich straight out of my hand. I _____ in shock.

My big brother looked at my empty hand and _____.

"Just look at your face!" he laughed.

"Leave me alone," I _____ angrily, but he just kept on laughing.

C Put these words in the order you would find them in a dictionary.

detail   dusty   dwell   door   damp   dare   dye   drop

1st <u>damp</u>   2nd _____   3rd _____   4th _____
5th _____   6th _____   7th _____   8th _____

Poetry Vocabulary and spelling • Student book page 140

Thesaurus work

A Use a **thesaurus** to match the words in the clouds to the word that they could replace. Fill in the lists below.

Clouds: shriek, yell, urge, implore, amble, traipse, sob, plead, bellow, request, weep, stroll, bawl, roar, stride, wail

walk	beg	cry	shout
____	____	____	____
____	____	____	____
____	____	____	____
____	____	____	____

B Choose one of the words from your lists in the previous exercise to replace the word in brackets and complete these sentences. Remember to use the past tense.

1 Leonard _____ (**walk**) home from school feeling happy that it was Friday.

2 "Please, please, please may I have a puppy," Kia _____ (**beg**) her mum.

3 "You are not going anywhere until you have cleaned your room," _____ (**shout**) my dad.

4 "You've eaten all my birthday cake," _____ (**cry**) my little sister.

COPYRIGHT OXFORD UNIVERSITY PRESS 2013. PHOTOCOPYING PROHIBITED

Poetry Vocabulary and spelling • Student book pages 140 and 141

Dictionary work and homonyms

A Look in the dictionary and find three different meanings of the word 'bark'.

Some homonyms are spelt differently but are pronounced the same.

Example: read, red

1 _____
2 _____
3 _____

B Find a homonym for these words from the words in the clouds on page 51.

raw _____

ball _____

whale _____

C Write a homonym to match these words. Use a dictionary to help you.

knew _____   hear _____   write _____

hole _____   meet _____   there _____

two _____   through _____ no _____

Writing a limerick

A Choose a word from the words in bold to fill the gaps and complete the two limericks.

1 **tomatoes   grass   packet   sorry
Leeds   lass*   seeds   covered**

[* **lass** is another word for girl]

There once was a young lady from _____,

who swallowed a _____ of _____.

Now this _____ young _____

is quite _____ in _____

but has all the _____ she needs.

2 **true   Peru   woke   terrible   shoe
perfectly   old   eating   fright
dreamt   night**

There was an _____ man of _____,

who _____ he was _____ a _____.

He _____ up one _____

with a _____ _____

and found out it was _____ _____.

Poetry Writing • Student book pages 142 and 143

B **Think of a way of completing this limerick using the rhyming words 'hour', 'flower' and 'weeds' at the end of the lines.**

There was a wee* toddler from Leeds,

who swallowed a packet of seeds.

_____

_____

_____

[*wee is another word for small.]

C **Choose *one* of the following opening lines and use it to write your own limerick.**

1 There once was a tortoise named Fred
2 There was a young lady called Sue
3 There was an old farmer from Wales
4 There was a poor girl in a hat

_____

_____

_____

_____

_____

Poetry Assessment

Self-assessment on my learning

Unit 9 Why do we laugh?

Name _____

Date _____

☺ I understand and can do this well.

😐 I understand but I am not confident.

☹ I don't understand and find this difficult.

Learning objective	☺	😐	☹
Reading poetry skills			
I can read a range of poetry.			
Writing skills			
I am getting better at choosing tenses.			
I am begining to use commas.			
Language skills			
I can use a dictionary to find the meaning of words.			
I can find examples of nouns and adjectives.			
I can find synonyms for words.			
I can use powerful adjectives and verbs.			
I can find words that have the same spelling but a different meaning.			

I would like more help with _____

_____

_____

Word cloud dictionary

Aa
adamantly *adverb* do or say something in a way that shows you are determined or have a strong opinion

address *noun* your address is where you live

adventure *noun* a strange, exciting or dangerous event or journey

air mail *noun* letters and parcels that are carried by aircraft

ajar *adjective* partly open

amusing *adjective* making you laugh or smile

Arctic *noun* the area round the North Pole

authority *noun* the power to give orders

Bb
boarding school *noun* a school where children are able to live during term time

burrow *verb* dig a hole under the ground

Cc
canoe *noun* a light, narrow boat that you move by using a paddle

cardboard *noun* very thick, strong paper

climber *noun* someone who climbs hills and mountains for sport

compost *noun* a mixture of rotten stalks, leaves and grass

creator *noun* someone who creates or makes something

creep *verb* move along quietly and slowly with the body close to the ground

Word Cloud dictionary

crumb noun a very tiny piece of bread or cake
culture noun all the traditions and customs of a group of people such as art, music, literature, science and learning
cyclist noun a person who rides a bicycle

Dd
danger noun the chance that something bad might happen or someone might get hurt
decoration noun an object that is added to make something look more beautiful or colourful
detective noun someone who looks at clues and tries to solve a mystery or find out who committed a crime
downstream adverb in the direction that a river or stream flows
drain noun a pipe or ditch for taking away waste, water or sewage

Ee
elastic band noun a band made of stretchy material, used to hold things in place
elegant adjective graceful or tasteful
enquiry noun a question you ask when you want information
exaggerate verb say that something is bigger, better or more important than it really is

Ff
festival noun a special time when people celebrate something
flavour noun the taste of something that you eat or drink

COPYRIGHT OXFORD UNIVERSITY PRESS 2013. PHOTOCOPYING PROHIBITED 57

frond *noun* a large leaf, which is made up of lots of smaller leaves, such as the leaf of a fern plant
frozen *adjective* something that has turned to ice
frustrate *verb* prevent someone from doing something or from succeeding in something

Gg
gasp *verb* breathe in suddenly when you are shocked or surprised
glue *noun* a sticky substance that you use for sticking or holding things together
greet *verb* welcome someone and say hello to them
grill *noun* a device for cooking food, which uses a flame or a glowing element
grizzle *verb* sulk, grumble or whine
grub *noun* an animal that looks like a small worm and will become an insect when it is an adult

Hh
haul *verb* pull or drag something along
howl *verb* make a long, high sound, like the sound of an animal crying or a strong wind blowing
hunt *verb* chase and kill animals for food or as a sport

Ii
instruction *noun* an order or piece of information that tells you what to do

Jj
joke *noun* something you say or do to make people laugh
journey *noun* when you go on a journey, you travel somewhere

Word Cloud dictionary

Kk
kiln *noun* a type of oven or furnace

Ll
ladder *noun* a tall frame you can climb to reach something high up
laugh *verb* make a noise or sound that shows you are happy or think something is funny
legend *noun* an old story that has been handed down from the past
limerick *noun* a funny poem with five lines and a strong rhythm
loom *noun* a machine for weaving cloth

Mm
Maori *noun* a member of the aboriginal people of New Zealand
master *noun* a male teacher
mistake *noun* something that is wrong
mystery *noun* something strange and puzzling that you do not understand

Nn
nibble *verb* take tiny bites of something
noise *noun* a sound that you can hear

Oo
overjoyed *adjective* very happy or delighted

Pp
pant *verb* take short, quick breaths because you have been moving quickly
peck *verb* the motion a bird makes with its beak to touch something or pick it up

pedestrian *noun* someone who is walking along the street

peer *verb* look at someone or something closely or with difficulty

pipe cleaner *noun* a small wire covered in soft material, used to hold things together in craft

post office *noun* a place where you post letters and parcels and can buy stamps

publish *verb* print and sell a book or magazine

puff *verb* breathe in and out quickly because you have been running or exercising

Rr

ranch *noun* a large farm where a lot of sheep, cows or horses are kept

rattly *adjective* making a series of quick, short sounds like a rattle

remote *adjective* a place that is far away from towns and cities

reward *noun* something that is given to someone because they have done something good or helpful

rock *verb* move gently backwards and forwards or from side to side

rush *verb* run or do something quickly

Ss

safety *noun* keeping safe and away from danger

satchel *noun* a bag you wear over your shoulder or on your back, especially for carrying books to and from school

scent *noun* a nice smell or perfume

scissors *noun* a tool that you use for cutting paper or cloth

Word Cloud dictionary

scrape *verb* rub something against a rough, hard or sharp object

shear *verb* cut hair very short or cut the wool of a sheep

shiny *adjective* glossy or polished; bright

shrug *verb* lift your shoulders up and down, usually to show that you do not know something or do not care about it

slip *verb* slide or accidentally fall over

smirking *adjective* smiling in a silly or smug way

smug *adjective* very pleased with yourself

snare *noun* a trap for catching animals

snatch *verb* take hold of something quickly and unexpectedly

sniff *verb* breathe in air noisily through the nose, or to smell something by sniffing

spring *verb* move quickly or suddenly

squeal *verb* shout or cry out in a high voice

stable *noun* a building in which horses are kept

stamp album *noun* a book in which collectors of postage stamps can display and store their stamps

steal *verb* take something from someone without permission

struggle *verb* try to get free, or find something difficult

swishing *noun* the quick movement of something through the air, which makes a soft sound

Tt

thief *noun* someone who steals things

tights *noun* clothing which fits tightly over the legs and lower body

tradition *noun* something people have done in the same way for a very long time as part of their culture

trance *noun* a dreamy or unconscious state, as if you are sleeping

Word Cloud dictionary

trickle *verb* flow slowly or thinly
truly *adverb* do something in a true or faithful way
two-way radio *noun* a radio through which you can communicate in both directions

Uu
underground *adjective* under the ground

Ww
warning *noun* something said or written to warn someone
weave *verb* make cloth from threads or a basket from reeds or cane
whistle *verb* make a high sound by blowing air through your lips
whopper *noun* anything unusually big of its kind
windmill *noun* a building with large sails that move in the wind and use the power of the wind to make energy
withdraw *verb* take something away take it back
wobbly *adjective* unsteady

62 COPYRIGHT OXFORD UNIVERSITY PRESS 2013. PHOTOCOPYING PROHIBITED

100 High frequency words

A
a
about
all
an
and
are
as
asked
at

B
back
be
big
but
by

C
called
came
can

children
come
could

D
dad
day
do
don't
down

F
for
from

G
get
go
got

H
had
have
he

help
her
here
him
his
house

I
I
I'm
if
in
into
is
it
it's

J
just

L
like
little

look
looked

M
made
make
me
Mr
Mrs
mum
my

N
no
not
now

O
of
off
oh
old
on

100 High frequency words

one	so	this	we
out	some	time	went
P	**T**	to	were
people	that	too	what
put	the	**U**	when
S	their	up	will
said	them	**V**	with
saw	then	very	**Y**
see	there	**W**	you
she	they	was	your

64 COPYRIGHT OXFORD UNIVERSITY PRESS 2013. PHOTOCOPYING PROHIBITED

100 High frequency words

A Find the nouns, verbs, adjectives and adverbs in the list of high frequency words and complete the chart below (some words might go into more than one group).

noun	verb	adjective	adverb

100 High frequency words

B Use a dictionary to help you find three words from the list of high frequency words that can be used in more than one word category. Then make sentences to show the different meanings. *Example*: saw

saw/*noun* I used the saw to cut off the branch from the tree.

saw/*verb* I saw a really interesting programme about dolphins last night.

1 _____

2 _____

3 _____

100 High frequency words

C. Complete this table using the nouns from the list of high frequency words.

singular	plural
dad	dads

100 High frequency words

A Look at the verbs in the list of high frequency words. Divide them into the following two groups.

present	past
come	asked

B Choose five of the present tense verbs above and change them into the past tense. Then use the verbs in a sentence.

Example: come

My friend **came** to my house to ask if I wanted to go to the park with him.

1 _____
2 _____
3 _____
4 _____
5 _____

C Find the two question words in the list of high frequency words and use each of them to write a question about your favourite animal.

1 _____
2 _____

New Word List

Home language(s)	English

New Word List

Home language(s)	English